This book is dedicated to all the folks at Martin Luther Lutheran Church, Giddings, Texas, who first memorized the words herein and especially to the pastors at the time, Charles Ager and Patti Luebben, who took a chance with letting this odd theater guy take over Lent, 1990.

Watch And Pray

Meditations In Dramatic Form For The Season Of Lent

NEIL ELLIS ORTS

CSS Publishing Company, Inc., Lima, Ohio

WATCH AND PRAY

Library of Congress Cataloging-in-Publication Data

Orts, Neil Ellis, 1963-
    Watch and pray : meditations in dramatic form for the season of Lent / Neil Ellis Orts.
        p.   cm.
    ISBN 0-7880-0390-9 (pbk.)
    1. Lent. 2. Worship programs. 3. Drama in public worship. 4. Lent—Meditations.
I. Title.
BV85.O78   1996
242'.34—dc20
                                                        95-25340
                                                        CIP

ISBN: 0-7880-0390-9
PRINTED IN U.S.A.

Table Of Contents

Guidelines

- Speeches are numbered rather than divided into parts. This allows for as many people to participate as are willing to do so. It also allows for any age or gender ratio. Simply divide the speeches among your volunteers. Random order is more interesting than repeating a set order.

- Anything written in ALL CAPS is to be said in unison by the whole cast.

- Movement should be simple and direct. As the lines seldom require specific movement, anything that looks good in the worship space is generally acceptable. Some thought should be given as to when the lines suggest that the cast should be close to each other and when they might be dispersed, when a line might be more effective when said from the back of the church or by the baptismal font.

- The scriptures are to be read. This allows for the participation of those who are uncomfortable with memorization. Also, note the use of the Gospel responses (Glory to you, O Lord). The congregation will likely join in with the cast on their own, but if not, encourage them to do so. Then the whole congregation takes part in the "drama," even if it is on a limited basis.

- Although no specific costumes are required, the cast should keep in mind the season. Dark pants or skirt (black, purple, navy) with a white shirt are appropriate. Reds, yellows, pinks and the like should be avoided.

- The suggested Psalms may be used within the "play" or not. The first time these were used, the Psalm was spoken with the congregation before the final "WATCH AND PRAY." (One cast member would simply announce, "Let us join together in praying Psalm 139.")

- These meditations are mostly a framework for a congregation to build upon. While they were written to be memorized by a cast, they may be presented as readers' theater. They have also been used as an opening devotion for a college student group's weekly meetings during Lent. It is conceivable that music, visuals (slides or video), or dance might be used with these meditations. They are limited only by a congregation's resources and imagination. Only one word of caution: Each week's service comes up very quickly, so don't become so elaborate that you lack sufficient time to put it together. But think about that after you've brainstormed the possibilities!

- The scripture readings are taken from *The Good News Bible* (Today's English Version).

- The readings for Ash Wednesday are as prescribed by the lectionary in the *Lutheran Book Of Worship*. The Maundy Thursday readings draw upon all the readings from the three-year cycle, conforming to none of the years solely. The readings for the Wednesdays in between were chosen according to the theme of the week, with attention paid to the weekly and daily lectionaries where possible.

Ash Wednesday
Watch And Pray

Readings
Joel 2:12-19
2 Corinthians 5:20—6:2
Matthew 6:1-6, 16-21
Psalm 51

1 — WATCH AND PRAY.

2 — These are the words of our Savior to his disciples as he went to pray in the garden. It was the night he was betrayed to his enemies.

3 — WATCH AND PRAY.

4 — This is our call to you this season of Lent, as we reflect once again upon that final week Christ walked the earth.

5 — WATCH AND PRAY.

6 — What are we watching for?

7 — What are we praying for?

8 — Let us first look at the significance of Lent.

9 — Lent is a word with origins in Old English, a word for spring. It possibly comes from a word meaning lengthen, as spring is the time when the days get longer.

10 — Historically, the forty days before Easter were used as a time of instruction and fasting for new converts who would be receiving baptism on Easter Sunday.

11 — In the Anglo world, this period was given the name Lent.

12 — Why is such a solemn time given a name for spring, the season of renewal? Shouldn't this be a time of celebration?

13 — That is where Easter comes in. There is our celebration of spring, of warmer days and the renewing earth.

14 — Consider the farmer. Before he can celebrate the greening of his fields, he must work the soil and plant the seed.

15 — He has to overcome many obstacles for a good harvest. He is dependent upon the richness of the soil, the timing of the rains, and the diligence of his own hard work.

16 — Spiritually, we spend the forty days of Lent in solemn reflection in order to appreciate more fully the Resurrection of Easter.

17 — The solemnity of Lent perhaps can be seen as planting the seeds for the Resurrection.

18 — WATCH AND PRAY.

19 — Spring is also the earth turning its back on winter, the season of sleep or death.

20 — Lent has traditionally been a time of repentance and the word "repent," in Christian terms, means to turn away and reject sin and death and accept salvation and life.

21 — When we repent, we are as if born again, just as the earth is reborn each spring.

22 — WATCH AND PRAY.

23 — A reading from the book of Joel, the prophet.

> *"But even now," says the Lord, "repent sincerely and return to me with fasting and weeping and mourning. Let your broken heart show your sorrow; tearing your clothes is not enough."*
>
> *Come back to the Lord your God. He is kind and full of mercy; he is patient and keeps his promise; he is always ready to forgive and not punish. Perhaps the Lord your God will change his mind and bless you with abundant crops. Then you can offer him grain and wine.*
>
> *Blow the trumpet on Mount Zion; give orders for a fast and call an assembly! Gather the people together; prepare them for a sacred meeting; bring the old people; gather the children and the babies, too. Even newly married couples must leave their homes and come. The priests, serving the Lord between the altar and the entrance of the Temple, must weep and pray: "Have pity on your people, Lord. Do not let other nations despise us and mock us by saying, 'Where is your God?'"*
>
> *Then the Lord showed concern for his land; he had mercy on his people. He answered them: "Now I am going to give you grain and wine and olive oil, and you will be satisfied. Other nations will no longer despise you."*

Here ends the reading.

24 — Joel calls for repentance, not just from one person, or from one class of people.

25 — God wants everyone to turn to him.

26 — From babies to the elderly.

27 — Newlyweds must leave their new home, Joel says.

28 — All people must put aside their concerns and turn to God.

29 — Even enemies must put aside their differences and, together, turn to God.

30 — WATCH AND PRAY.

31 — Joel made a connection between repentance and God's gifts from the earth.

(32 through 39 spoken antiphonally)

32 — SPRING IS THE TIME OF PLANTING CROPS.

33 — AND OF REPENTANCE.

34 — SO WE CAN CELEBRATE THE RENEWAL OF THE EARTH AND ITS BOUNTY

35 — AND THE RESURRECTION.

36 — BECAUSE THE TIME WILL COME WHEN THINGS WILL NOT GROW

37 — AND THINGS WILL DIE

38 — AND WE WILL NEED THE HOPE OF NEW CROPS

39 — AND THE RESURRECTION.

40 — "Watch and pray," the Master said.

41 — We are watching for the Resurrection.

42 — We are praying for new life.

43 — What else? Is this all we are to pray about?

44 — There is a multitude to pray about.

45 — But this is where we start.

46 — WATCH AND PRAY.

47 — A reading from the second letter to the Corinthians from Paul the Apostle.

> *We plead on Christ's behalf: let God change you from enemies into his friends! Christ was without sin but for our sake God made him share our sin in order that in union with him we might share the righteousness of God.*
>
> *In our work together with God, then, we beg you who have received God's grace not to let it be wasted. Hear what God says: "When the time came for me to show you favor, I heard you; when the day arrived for me to save you, I helped you."*
>
> *Listen! This is the hour to receive God's favor; today is the day to be saved!*

Here ends the reading.

48 — Today is the day to be saved.

49 — We look to the resurrection but today, this hour, is the time to receive salvation.

50 — This is the glorious grace of God, that we may repent at any time, that we may receive salvation at any hour.

51 — But what is this Paul said? Let God change us from enemies into his friends?

52 — Yes, for as long as we are not for God, we are against him. We are not his friends until we accept his loving gift of salvation.

53 — So we are his enemies from birth.

54 — Sinners from our mothers' wombs.

55 — This is why we must repent, turn away from what our human nature desires and turn to God's will.

56 — Turn from being enemies to being friends with each other and with God.

57 — WATCH AND PRAY.

58 — In the context of the scripture, Christ was telling his disciples to watch for the enemies, the soldiers that would be coming to arrest him.

59 — And Christ said, "... pray so you do not fall into temptation."

60 — This is hard to understand. What did Jesus mean by that?

61 — Pray, maybe, that they do not run as they all did?

62 — Pray, perhaps, that they are not tempted to attack the enemy as Peter did?

63 — Or pray that they do not fall into the temptation to become traitors as Judas did?

64 — What are we praying for?

65 — Maybe the same thing we watch for: our enemies.

66 — WATCH AND PRAY.

67 — There is a tradition for Lent that would have us concentrate on three things: almsgiving, prayer, and fasting.

68 — *(Reader should motion for congregation to stand.)* A reading from the Holy Gospel according to Saint Matthew.

69 — GLORY TO YOU, O LORD.

70 — *Make certain you do not perform your religious duties in public so that people will see what you do. If you do these things publicly, you will not have any reward from your Father in heaven.*

So when you give to a needy person, do not make a big show of it, as the hypocrites do in the houses of worship and on the streets. They do it so that people will praise them. I assure you, they have already been paid in full. But when you help a needy person, do it in such a way that even your closest friend will not know about it. Then it will be a private matter. And your Father, who sees what you do in private, will reward you.

When you pray, do not be like the hypocrites! They love to stand up and pray in the houses of worship and on the street corners, so that everyone will see them. I assure you, they have already been paid in full. But when you pray, go to your room, close the door, and pray to your Father, who is unseen. And your Father, who sees what you do in private, will reward you.

And when you fast, do not put on a sad face as the hypocrites do. They neglect their appearance so that everyone will see that they are fasting. I assure you, they have already been paid in full. When you go without food, wash your face and comb your hair, so that others cannot know that you are fasting — only your Father, who sees what you do in private, will reward you.

The Gospel of the Lord.

71 — PRAISE TO YOU, O CHRIST.

72 — Our Lord has given us the standard to perform these duties.

73 — If we give to charity to be called great philanthropists, is that really charity?

74 — THIS IS NOT THE WAY OF CHRIST.

75 — If we pray with loud praises and obvious gestures in order to be called great religious people, is that really prayer?

76 — THIS IS NOT THE WAY OF CHRIST.

77 — If we fast to be recognized as great holy people, is that true fasting?

78 — THIS IS NOT THE WAY OF CHRIST.

79 — The way of Christ is to give, pray, and fast so that we grow as children of God.

80 — So that we would be able to bear a cross and pray for the ones who nailed us there.

81 — WATCH AND PRAY

82 — for our enemies.

83 — Renewal is the word.

84 — Rebirth.

85 — We must be born again.

86 — This is what we hope to receive this Lent.

87 — We must be renewed so we can pray with Stephen,

88 — "LORD, DO NOT HOLD THIS SIN AGAINST THEM."

89 — This prayer is hard.

90 — It takes a lot to pray it.

91 — It takes soul-searching and self-knowledge, so we are secure in ourselves and in our faith.

92 — It takes our repentance, for we must see our own sin to have compassion for those who sin against us.

93 — It takes growth, the willingness to grow in faith, not to settle for the *status quo* of our soul.

94 — It takes patience to trust that God is in control in times of suffering.

95 — It takes self-discipline, self-control to keep ourselves from rash behavior.

96 — And it takes courage. Courage to accept our shortcomings, to accept our trials, to accept our cross.

97 — We will accept the ashes of Ash Wednesday and admit that we are also ashes.

98 — And we will watch and pray

99 — for our enemies.

100 — So that, like the mythological phoenix, we will also rise from the ashes to renewed life in Christ.

101 — WATCH AND PRAY.

102 — We are on our way to the cross.

Self-knowledge

Readings
Exodus 3:12-15
1 Corinthians 2:6-12
Luke 18:9-14
Psalm 139

1 — WATCH AND PRAY.

2 — Since Adam was formed from the dust, there has been change.

3 — Kingdoms have risen and fallen.

4 — Cultures have flourished and disappeared.

5 — Science has been learned and forgotten.

6 — Art has been created and destroyed.

7 — And in the midst of all the changes, humankind has forever searched for meaning.

8 — All the philosophers, all the artists,

9 — all the rulers and politicians,

10 — the laborers and the tradesmen,

11 — all have desired purpose.

12 — Regardless of the culture, individuals have struggled with this one basic question:

13 — Who am I?

14 — WATCH AND PRAY.

15 — A reading from the book of Exodus.

> *But Moses replied, "When I go to the Israelites and say to them, 'The God of your ancestors sent me to you,' they will ask me, 'What is his name?' So what can I tell them?"*
>
> *God said, "I am who I am. You must tell them: 'The one who is called I AM has sent me to you.' Tell the Israelites that I, the Lord, the God of their ancestors, the God of Abraham, Isaac, and Jacob, have sent you to them. This is my name forever; this is what all future generations are to call me."*

Here ends the reading.

16 — God, in his holy perfection, knew the answer to Moses' question.

17 — We rely on names to identify ourselves. God simply is.

18 — "I am who I am," God answered.

19 — We are not God, but we are made in his image.

20 — Why, then, is it so hard for us to answer the same question so simply?

21 — Why are we so insecure in who we are?

22 — WATCH AND PRAY.

23 — A reading from the first letter to the Corinthians from Paul the Apostle.

> *Yet I do proclaim a message of wisdom to those who are spiritually mature. But it is not the wisdom that belongs to this world — powers that are losing their power. The wisdom I proclaim is God's secret wisdom, which is hidden from humankind, but which he had already chosen for our glory even before the world was made. None of the rulers of this world knew this wisdom. If they had known it, they would not have crucified the Lord of glory.*
>
> *However, as the scripture says, "What no one ever saw or heard, what no one ever thought could happen, is the very thing God prepared for those who love him."*
>
> *But it was to us that God made known his secret by means of his spirit. The Spirit searches everything, even the hidden depths of God's purposes. It is only a person's own spirit within him that knows all about God. We have not received this world's spirit; instead, we have received the Spirit sent by God, so that we may know all that God has given us.*

Here ends the reading.

24 — Only God's Spirit knows all about God,

25 — just as only our spirits know all about us.

26 — But if our spirits know all about us, then why do so many people agonize over the question of identity?

27 — If only we were a more spiritual people.

28 — But we are in the world and forget that we have received the Spirit of God, not the spirit of the world.

29 — So we spend our time putting our trust in material things.

30 — We begin to identify ourselves with what we have, how we dress, the work we do.

31 — We take pride in our riches, or else wish for them.

32 — And we play at being spiritual, occasionally using religious terms to identify ourselves.

33 — And if we imagine ourselves especially spiritual, we will attach ourselves to a spiritual leader and follow this leader wherever he or she might lead.

(The following four lines are a dialogue between only two cast members.)

34 — Don't you love to listen to Pastor Goodenlaud preach?

35 — Oh, yes. I am always so blessed when I hear him speak.

36 — It's that voice. So commanding. Why, Pastor Goodenlaud could convert Satan himself.

37 — I just know I'd be lost without him.

38 — But take away this leader and within weeks we'll be dancing around a metal cow.

39 — Or some other cultural icon.

40 — Replacing one idol with another.

41 — Search yourself. Know yourself.

42 — WATCH AND PRAY.

43 — It is a well-documented fact that religion spreads in poor populations.

44 — People in affluent countries often feel like they don't need religion.

45 — The church has nothing to offer them.

46 — But in poor populations, the people do not have fine clothes, fancy cars, or beautiful homes to hold onto.

47 — Stripped of all material wealth, the poor are the most likely to reach into the air and grab hold of the only tangible thing there.

48 — God.

49 — What do you cling to?

50 — WATCH AND PRAY.

51 — Jesus knew who he was and he knew his Father.

52 — They share the same Spirit.

53 — How else could Christ have entered Jerusalem that Sunday, knowing that in the week that was to follow, everything would be stripped from his being?

54 — Even his life.

55 — And still have the grace to pray for his enemies as he hung,

56 — broken, bleeding,

57 — dying on a cross.

58 — Who among us, with our cluttered, sinful souls, could do likewise?

59 — WATCH AND PRAY.

60 — A reading from the Holy Gospel according to Saint Luke.

61 — GLORY TO YOU, O LORD.

62 — *Jesus also told this parable to people who were sure of their goodness and despised everybody else. "Once there were two men who went up to the Temple to pray: one was a Pharisee, the other a tax collector. The Pharisee stood apart by himself and prayed, 'I thank you that I am not like that tax collector over there. I fast two days a week, and I give you one tenth of all my income.' But the tax collector stood at a distance and would not even raise his face to heaven, but beat upon his breast and said, 'God, have pity on me, a sinner!' I tell you," Jesus said, "the tax collector, and not the Pharisee, was in the right with God when he went home. For everyone who makes himself great will be humbled, and everyone who humbles himself will be made great.*

The Gospel of the Lord.

63 — PRAISE TO YOU, O CHRIST.

64 — This is a familiar story. The Pharisee, the respectable citizen, is held up by Jesus as a poor example.

65 — Pride is the sin, humility, the missing virtue.

66 — Rather than beg forgiveness for his sin, the Pharisee compared himself to the tax collector and found his own the smaller sin.

67 — How often do we do this?

68 — Okay! I lied a little. But nobody got hurt as when some people sin.

69 — Sure, I shoplift a small item here and there, but it's not like I'm a bank robber.

70 — Yeah, yeah. So I sometimes juggle the books in my favor. You act like I killed somebody.

71 — Thank you, God, that I am not like all the thieves, murderers, and rapists in the world.

(Unison, only two or three cast members.)

72 — THANK YOU THAT MINE ARE SMALL SINS,

(Unison, the whole company.)

73 — SINS THAT ALLOW ME TO KEEP MY PLACE OF RESPECT IN MY BUSINESS, HOME, AND CHURCH.

(After taking a moment to realize what they have prayed.)

74 — WATCH AND PRAY.

75 — The Pharisee looked on the outside and found his actions to be good and to the letter of the law.

76 — The tax collector looked inside and found himself sinful and in need of God's mercy.

77 — Let us do like the tax collector. Let us look inside and see our sin.

78 — Let us look within and face our own darkness.

79 — But do not stop there lest you should die in despair. Look past the darkness.

80 — If you believe in Christ and accept his salvation, you will find beneath the darkness of sin a Light living there, a Light no darkness has ever overcome.

81 — There you will find Christ who has claimed you as his temple.

82 — Know that what good you do comes from this Light that lives in darkness. Invite that Light to guide your life through the darkness that surrounds you.

83 — LET YOUR LIGHT SO SHINE BEFORE OTHERS THAT THEY MAY SEE YOUR GOOD WORKS AND GLORIFY YOUR FATHER IN HEAVEN.

84 — Christ knew himself. He was sure of his place in his father's Kingdom. It was this security that allowed him to pray for his enemies.

85 — Know yourself.

86 — Know that beyond your material wealth,

87 — beyond your physical appearance,

88 — even beyond your name,

89 — know that you have identity.

90 — And no one, no enemy however great, can take this from you.

91 — Truly and profoundly, you are a child of God.

92 — WATCH AND PRAY.

93 — As we approach the cross.

Third Wednesday in Lent
Repentance

Readings
Jeremiah 8:4-7
Romans 5:6-11
Luke 13:1-5
Psalm 46

1 — Repent! For the kingdom of God is at hand!

2 — Repent!

3 — Repent!

4 — Turn from your sin and repent!

5 — Each year we hear these cries.

6 — Each Lenten season reminds us that we are sinners and need God's salvation.

7 — Last week, we called for all to examine themselves,

8 — to look into the darkness of their own souls.

9 — But repentance is more than feeling regret or remorse for our sin.

10 — Repentance is actively turning away from that sin and accepting the challenge to live a godly life.

11 — We say yes to the challenge when we turn away from our human nature and respond to God's gift of grace.

12 — But we do not repent once and go on to live godly lives.

13 — We repent daily.

14 — We turn to God daily for his grace to carry on in our human weakness.

15 — Each day we need to be born again to accept this challenge.

16 — WATCH AND PRAY.

17 — A reading from the book of Jeremiah, the prophet.

The Lord told me to say to his people, "When someone falls down, doesn't he get back up? If someone misses the road, doesn't he turn back? Why then, my people, do you turn away from me without ever turning back? You cling to your idols and refuse to return to me. I listened carefully, but you did not speak the truth. Not one of you has been sorry for his wickedness; not one of you has asked, 'What have I done wrong?' Everyone keeps on going his own way, like a horse rushing into battle. Even storks know when it is time to return; doves, swallows, and thrushes know when it is time to migrate. But, my people, you do not know the laws by which I rule you."

Here ends the reading.

18 — In baptism, we receive a promise.

19 — A promise of grace.

20 — In Adam and Eve, we received a worldly nature that rejected God and his creation.

21 — But through baptism, we drown the old nature and receive a new nature.

22 — We become new creations.

23 — We are sealed by the Holy Spirit and marked with the Cross of Christ forever.

24 — We often forget this promise, however.

25 — It is much easier to follow the path of Adam than to follow the path of Christ.

26 — That is why we have said we must actively turn away from sin.

27 — That is why we say we must repent daily.

28 — And Jeremiah tells us what repentance is:

29 — Repentance is knowing that we have fallen and need to get back up.

30 — Repentance is knowing when we have taken the wrong road and need to turn back and find the right one.

31 — Birds know when to return in the spring,

32 — and Lent is our season to return to our God.

33 — WATCH AND PRAY.

34 — A reading from Paul's letter to the Romans.

For when we were still helpless, Christ died for the wicked at the time that God chose. It is a difficult thing for someone to die for a righteous person. It may even be that someone might dare to die for a good person. But God has shown us how much he loves us — it was while we were sinners that Christ died for us! By his sacrificial death we are now put right with God; how much more, then, will we be saved by him from God's anger! We were God's enemies, but he made us his friends through the death of his Son. Now that we are God's friends, how much more will we be saved by Christ's life! But that is not all; we rejoice because of what God has done through our Lord Jesus Christ, who has now made us God's friends.

Here ends the reading.

35 — When we turn to Christ, he accepts us, even though we were once his enemies.

36 — Jesus takes us in when he should want nothing to do with us.

37 — Are we to ignore his example?

38 — Jesus prayed for the ones who nailed him to the cross.

39 — How many of us would pray for a person holding a gun to our heart?

40 — Of course, this is the obvious scenario when we speak of enemies. We imagine a violent or brutal crime.

41 — But few of us ever meet such a frightening situation.

42 — In fact, some of us may feel we have no enemies at all.

43 — But we do have enemies if we include all the people we simply don't get along with.

44 — If we consider these people enemies, we must realize that what makes two people enemies has more to do with the sinfulness of our human nature than with the righteousness of one over the other.

45 — We must learn to admit that we are not wholly righteous and those who oppose us are not wholly unrighteous.

46 — We do not have the ability nor the right to judge another.

47 — All we can do is be sure of our own sincere attempts at repentance.

48 — From there we must trust God's grace.

49 — WATCH AND PRAY.

50 — A reading from the Holy Gospel according to Saint Luke.

51 — GLORY TO YOU, O LORD.

52 — *At that time some people were there who told Jesus about the Galileans whom Pilate had killed while they were offering sacrifices to God. Jesus answered them, "Because those Galileans were killed in that way, do you think it proves that they were worse sinners than all other Galileans? No indeed! And I tell you that if you do not turn from your sins, you will all die as they did. What about those eighteen people in Siloam who were killed when the tower fell on them? Do you suppose this proves that they were worse than all the other people living in Jerusalem? No indeed! And I tell you that if you do not turn from your sins, you will all die as they did."*

The Gospel of the Lord.

53 — PRAISE TO YOU, O CHRIST.

54 — The lesson of the Gospel is clear.

55 — God's judgment falls on all people. His grace is equally distributed as well.

56 — Those who suffer are not in punishment,

57 — and those who lead lives free of tragedy are not necessarily godly people.

58 — But all are in need of God's loving salvation.

59 — All are in need of repentance,

60 — our enemies

61 — and ourselves.

62 — For none of us would be found worthy in and of our own deeds.

63 — Praise God for the means to salvation.

64 — Praise God for a refuge from the storms of sin and death.

65 — Praise God for the sacrifice of his Son, who calls us to turn and be with him.

66 — WATCH AND PRAY.

67 — We can see the cross.

Fourth Wednesday in Lent
Growth

Readings
Jeremiah 18:1-11
1 Corinthians 12:4-11
Mark 4:1-9
Psalm 1

1 — WATCH AND PRAY.

2 — We are planting seeds.

3 — We are cultivating the soil and praying for a good growth season this spring.

4 — We look forward to celebrating the green fields and growing crops.

5 — But for now, we are in the midst of solemn work, the almost joyless task of turning soil.

6 — We are planting seeds.

7 — We are the seeds.

8 — You and I are he and she.

9 — We are entering the cold, dark ground that is the Lenten season.

10 — And we are struggling to swell and burst with new life.

11 — As we grow and before we bear fruit, we will come up against many obstacles.

12 — The dirt that covers us,

13 — the rains that fall,

14 — The heat from the sun.

15 — Each is an enemy to our growth,

16 — and each is necessary.

17 — WATCH AND PRAY.

18 — A reading from the book of Jeremiah, the prophet.

The Lord said to me, "Go down to the potter's house, where I will give you my message." So I went there and saw the potter working at his wheel. Whenever a piece of pottery turned out imperfect, he would take the clay and make it into something else.

Then the Lord said to me, "Don't I have the right to do with you people of Israel what the potter did with the clay? You are in my hands just like clay in the potter's hands. If at any time I say that I am going to uproot, break down, or destroy any nation or kingdom, but then that nation turns from its evil, I will not do what I said I would. On the other hand, if I say that I am going to plant, or build up any nation or kingdom, but then that nation disobeys me and does evil, I will not do what I said I would. Now then, tell the people of Judah and of Jerusalem that I am making plans against them and getting ready to punish them. Tell them to stop living sinful lives — to change their ways and the things they are doing."

Here ends the reading.

19 — Have you ever tried to make a clay pot?

20 — Or paint a picture?

21 — Or sew a shirt?

22 — Or build a house?

23 — At times it seems as if the materials have minds of their own and refuse to be shaped into the desired objects.

24 — But as the creators of the objects, we are able to take them apart and start over again.

25 — We are like a house.

26 — We, too, have minds of our own and refuse to be shaped as desired by our Creator.

27 — We wish to create ourselves in our own image.

28 — But unless we learn to yield to our Creator's will, we will ultimately destroy ourselves.

29 — WATCH AND PRAY.

30 — A reading from the first letter to the Corinthians from Paul the Apostle.

There are different kinds of spiritual gifts, but the same Spirit gives them. There are different ways of serving, but the same Lord is served. There are different abilities to perform service, but the same God gives ability to everyone for their particular service. The Spirit's presence is shown for the good of all. The spirit gives one person a message full of wisdom, while to another person the same Spirit gives a message full of knowledge. One and the same Spirit gives faith to one person, while to another person he gives the power to heal. The Spirit gives one person the power to work miracles; to another, the gift of speaking God's message; and to yet another, the ability to tell the difference between the gifts that come from the Spirit and those that do not. To one person he gives the ability to speak in strange tongues, and to another he gives the ability to explain what is said. But it is one and the same Spirit who does all this; as he wishes, he gives a different gift to each person.

Here ends the reading.

31 — One Spirit.

32 — One Spirit gives us our gifts.

33 — We are given gifts to complement each other, not to be like each other.

34 — We are not whole in and of ourselves.

35 — A stone by itself is just a stone, but stones put together can build a house.

36 — We are living stones, building the church.

37 — What a grand and glorious building this church would be,

38 — how brilliantly it would display God's glory to the world,

39 — if it weren't for the stones desiring to be something else.

40 — It starts as a doorway wishes to be an altar.

41 — Or a window wishes to be a floor.

42 — "I'm no good at letting people in," says the doorway. "I am better suited to have the gifts laid upon me."

43 — "What good is a window?" asks the window. "Better I should be a plush, carpeted floor for the worshippers to kneel upon."

44 — And soon, the different parts of the church are arguing and fighting.

45 — Each part denying its gift in pursuit of another gift.

46 — But an altar cannot let in worshippers.

47 — And a floor lets in no light.

48 — And there is no need for the altar and door and floor and window to be enemies.

49 — There are different gifts to perform different tasks,

50 — but one spirit gives the gifts.

51 — WATCH AND PRAY.

52 — The Holy Gospel according to Saint Mark.

53 — GLORY TO YOU, O LORD.

Again Jesus began to teach beside Lake Galilee. The crowd that gathered around him was so large that he got into a boat and sat in it. The boat was out in the water and the crowd stood on the shore at the water's edge. He used parables to teach them many things, saying to them:

"Listen! Once there was a man who went out to sow grain. As he scattered the seed in the field, some of it fell along the path, and the birds came and ate it up. Some of it fell on rocky ground, where there was little soil. The seeds soon sprouted, because the soil wasn't deep. Then, when the sun came up, it burned the young plants; and because the roots had not grown deep enough, the plants soon dried up. Some of the seed fell among thorn bushes, which grew up and choked the plants, and they didn't bear grain. But some seeds fell in good soil, and the plants sprouted, grew, and bore grain: some had thirty grains, others sixty, and others one hundred."

And Jesus concluded, "Listen, then, if you have ears!"

The Gospel of the Lord.

54 — PRAISE TO YOU, O CHRIST.

55 — We are the seeds,

56 — and we fall into good and bad soil.

57 — But unlike the seeds of the parable, if we find ourselves among weeds, then we can move.

58 — If we find ourselves lying in a rock bed, we can go to better soil.

59 — Even if we land in good soil, the way is not easy.

60 — But whatever the obstacles, we must decide to grow,

61 — for a good seed will not remain a good seed forever.

62 — Lest we become only a hollow shell, we must decide to sprout, bloom and bear fruit.

63 — And, of course, this is possible only by the grace of God.

64 — It is in the hands of the Master Craftsman who forms us that we take shape as the Body of Christ.

65 — It is with the help of the Creator who plants us that we overcome obstacles and grow.

66 — And so, we begin to work together as friends, not as enemies.

67 — so that we may one day see the church as a whole, not as individual stones.

68 — So that we may each bear fruit, according to our gifts.

69 — WATCH AND PRAY.

70 — As we draw near the cross.

Fifth Wednesday in Lent
Patience

Readings
Genesis 45:1-8
James 5:7-11
Mark 13:9-13
Psalm 130

1 — WATCH AND PRAY.

2 — The Christian faith is a waiting faith.

3 — Starting with our spiritual ancestors, the Israelites waited for a Messiah.

4 — For hundreds of years, the Israelites waited.

5 — When he did appear, he was rejected and killed by Jew and Gentile alike. He proved his divinity, however, by rising from the grave.

6 — When he ascended into heaven, he promised to return to take his followers with him.

7 — For the past two thousand years, we have been waiting.

8 — Looking for the return of our Lord, Jesus Christ.

9 — WATCH AND PRAY.

10 — We are an impatient people.

11 — What should take a year to achieve, we want in a day.

12 — And God save us from having to wait 10 years to accomplish a goal.

13 — But a thousand years are like a day for God.

14 — And what we endure today may only be leading us to fulfill God's larger purposes.

15 — We may not be able to understand our suffering in the present.

16 — Indeed, we may not understand it in this life.

17 — But we must have faith that what we endure is not in vain.

18 — WATCH AND PRAY.

19 — A reading from the book of Genesis.

> *Joseph was no longer able to control his feelings in front of his servants, so he ordered them all to leave the room. No one else was with him when Joseph told his brothers who he was. He cried with such loud sobs that the Egyptians heard it, and the news was taken to the king's palace. Joseph said to his brothers, "I am Joseph. Is my father still alive?" But when his brothers heard this, they were so terrified that they could not answer. Then Joseph said to them, "Please come closer." They did and he said, "I am your*

44

brother Joseph, whom you sold into Egypt. Now do not be upset or blame yourselves because you sold me here. It was really God who sent me ahead of you to save people's lives. This is only the second year of the famine in the land; there will be five more years in which there will be neither plowing nor reaping. God sent me ahead of you to rescue you in this amazing way and to make sure that you and your descendants survive. So it was not really you who sent me here, but God."

Here ends the reading.

20 — We have just heard the happy ending of the story of Joseph.

21 — God used the treachery of Joseph's brothers to preserve the line of Abraham.

22 — But consider how long this took.

23 — When Joseph was sold into slavery, he was taken to Egypt where he became Potiphar's servant.

24 — Potiphar's wife laid a scheme that put Joseph in prison for at least two years.

25 — Then Joseph was made governor over Egypt for the seven years of plenty, which the king had dreamed about.

26 — Now, at the end of the story, we find it is in the second year of famine that Joseph revealed himself to his brothers.

27 — That makes 11 known years from the beginning of the story to the end.

28 — When Joseph was sold into slavery, he did not know he would eventually save his family from famine.

29 — As a servant and later as a prisoner, he could not foresee his future as the governor of Egypt.

30 — Only God could work a plan of salvation within those circumstances.

31 — God can work such a plan within our circumstances as well.

32 — But we must be patient and trust God to work his plan in due time.

33 — WATCH AND PRAY.

34 — A reading from the Letter of James.

> *Be patient, then, my brothers, until the Lord comes. See how patient a farmer is as he waits for his land to produce precious crops. He waits patiently for the autumn and spring rains. You also must be patient. Keep your hopes high, for the day of the Lord's coming is near.*
>
> *Do not complain against one another, my brothers, so that God will not judge you. The Judge is near, ready to appear. My brothers, remember the prophets who spoke in the name of the Lord. Take them as examples of patient endurance under suffering. We call them happy because they endured. You have heard of Job's patience, and you know how the Lord provided for him in the end. For the Lord is full of mercy and compassion.*

Here ends the reading.

35 — The Lord blesses those who endure hardships for his sake.

36 — And whatever the hardships may be, we have been given hope.

37 — We have the cycles of nature to give us hope.

38 — We have been given the scriptures and the stories of the prophets to give us hope.

39 — And we have the example of our Savior, who endured great suffering so we could conquer death.

40 — Through his resurrection, we are given hope.

41 — WATCH AND PRAY.

42 — Christianity is full of paradox.

43 — Imagine having an electric chair as a symbol of eternal life.

44 — But it is a means of execution, the cross, that gives us hope for that life everlasting.

45 — We are instructed to keep this hope alive, to be joyful and faithful.

46 — But in the same breath we are warned of coming tribulation.

47 — Christ promises that his yoke is light.

48 — And he also calls us to take up our cross and follow him.

49 — WATCH AND PRAY.

50 — The Holy Gospel according to Saint Mark.

51 — GLORY TO YOU, O LORD.

52 — *And Jesus said to them, "You yourselves must watch out: you will be arrested and taken to court. You will be beaten in the synagogues; you will stand before rulers and kings for my sake and tell them the Good News. But before the end comes, the gospel may be preached to all peoples. And when you are arrested and taken to court, do not worry ahead of time about what you will say; when the time comes, say whatever is then given to you. For the words you speak will not be yours; they will come from the Holy Spirit. Men will hand over their own brothers to be put to death, and fathers will do the same to their children. Children will turn against their parents and have them put to death. Everyone will hate you because of me. But whoever holds out to the end will be saved.*

The Gospel of the Lord.

53 — PRAISE TO YOU, O CHRIST.

54 — Jesus, in this gospel reading, is clearly defining what it means to be his disciples.

55 — If we follow him faithfully, he will save us from our sin and death.

56 — But he also promises that, because of that faith, we will have many enemies.

57 — When we are persecuted because of our faith, we are to preach the Good News to our enemies and pray for them as Jesus did on the cross.

58 — As we pray, we can remember Joseph, who did not understand why he was sold into slavery until 11 years later.

59 — Remember Job and his suffering. Remember God's blessing because of Job's faithfulness.

60 — Read the prophets and see how they endured ridicule and persecution.

61 — Have patience and wait for the fulfillment of God's promise.

62 — We are not alone in our suffering. We have hope.

63 — For whoever endures for Christ's sake shall be saved.

64 — WATCH AND PRAY.

65 — The cross is before us.

Discipline

Readings
Jeremiah 31:31-34
1 Corinthians 9:24-27
Matthew 25:14-30
Psalm 15

1 — WATCH AND PRAY.

2 — The season of Lent is nearly over.

3 — Five weeks ago, some of us may have made some promises to ourselves and to God.

4 — This year, I'm giving up chocolate for Lent.

5 — This year, I'm giving up television for Lent.

6 — This year, I'm reading a book on prayer for Lent.

7 — This year, I'm giving extra money to charity for Lent.

8 — These are the things we might choose for a Lenten discipline.

9 — Lenten disciplines help to remind us of the time of the year.

10 — They are supposed to help us focus on the suffering of Christ.

11 — By this point, however, many of us have given up our chosen disciplines.

12 — We are not here to make anyone feel guilty about setting aside his Lenten disciplines.

13 — In the greater scheme of things, these little promises probably don't mean that much to God anyway.

14 — But we do want to remind you of a greater promise.

15 — It is the covenant God has made with his people.

16 — WATCH AND PRAY.

17 — A reading from the book of Jeremiah.

> *The Lord says, "The time is coming when I will make a new covenant with the people of Israel and with the people of Judah. It will not be like the old covenant that I made with their ancestors when I took them by the hand and led them out of Egypt. Although I was like a husband to them, they did not keep that covenant. The new covenant that I will make with the people of Israel will be this: I will put my law within them and write it on their hearts. I will be their God, and they will be my people. None of them will have to teach his fellow countryman to know the Lord, because all will know me, from the least to the greatest. I will forgive their sins and I will no longer remember their wrongs. I, the Lord, have spoken."*

Here ends the reading.

18 — He will write his law on our hearts.

19 — And he will be our God and we will be his people.

20 — This is the covenant.

21 — This is the promise that God wants us to keep with him.

22 — But it is still a covenant that requires self-discipline.

23 — Even with God's law written on our hearts, we all too often choose to break this covenant.

24 — All too often, we reject what we know in our hearts is right.

25 — And we refuse to be God's people.

26 — WATCH AND PRAY.

27 — A reading from the first letter to the Corinthians from Paul the Apostle.

> *Surely you know that many runners take part in a race, but only one of them wins the prize. Run, then, in such a way as to win the prize. Every athlete in training submits to strict discipline, in order to be crowned with a wreath that will not last; but we do it for one that will last forever. That is why I run straight for the finish line; that is why I am like a boxer who does not waste his punches. I harden my body with blows and bring it under complete control, to keep myself from being disqualified after having called others to the contest.*

Here ends the reading.

28 — An Olympic-level athlete can be a marvel to behold.

29 — The grace of the gymnast.

30 — The strength of the power lifter.

31 — The endurance of the marathon runner.

32 — Few have the discipline required to achieve that level of performance.

33 — But this is how Paul challenges us in tonight's reading.

34 — We, as Christians, should train ourselves as an athlete trains for competition.

35 — We are challenged to submit to strict discipline in order to be crowned with a wreath that will last forever.

36 — The prize that only Christ can give.

37 — WATCH AND PRAY.

38 — Generally, in regards to a Lenten discipline, we try to correct a bad habit.

39 — But what is a bad habit?

40 — It is simply learned behavior that we perform over and over until it is second nature.

41 — A virtue is the same thing: a good behavior performed over and over until it, too, is second nature.

42 — Where we often fail in trying to overcome a bad habit is that we try to do too much too fast.

43 — But just as an Olympic runner didn't run a marathon the first day he ran, we shouldn't expect to correct a bad habit that may have developed over several years.

44 — The journey of 1,000 miles begins with the first step, says an ancient Chinese proverb. That first step is often fairly easy.

45 — But to take the second step requires discipline.

46 — As does each step that follows.

47 — WATCH AND PRAY.

48 — A reading from the Holy Gospel according to Saint Matthew.

49 — GLORY TO YOU, O LORD.

50 — *At that time the Kingdom of heaven will be like this. Once there was a man who was about to leave home on a trip; he called his servants and put them in charge of his property. He gave to each one according to his ability: to one he gave five thousand gold coins, to another he gave two thousand, and to another he gave one thousand. Then he left on his trip. The servant who had received five thousand coins went at once and invested his money and earned another five thousand. In the same way the servant who had received two thousand coins earned another two thousand. But the servant who had received one thousand coins went off, dug a hole in the ground, and hid his master's money.*

After a long time the master of those servants came back and settled accounts with them. The servant who had received five thousand coins came in and handed over the other five thousand. "You gave me five thousand coins, sir," he said. "Look! Here are another five thousand that I have earned." "Well done, you good and faithful servant!" said his master. "You have been faithful in managing small amounts, so I will put you in charge of large amounts. Come on in and share my happiness!" Then the servant who had been given two thousand coins came in and said, "You gave me two thousand coins, sir. Look! Here are another two thousand that I have earned." "Well done, you good and faithful servant!" said his master. "You have been faithful in managing small amounts, so I will put you in charge of large amounts. Come on in and share my happiness!" Then the servant who had received one thousand coins came in and said, "Sir, I know you are a hard man; you reap harvests where you did not scatter seed. I was afraid, so I went off and hid your money in the ground. Look! Here is what belongs to you." "You bad and lazy servant!" his master said. "You knew, did you, that I reap harvests where I did not plant, and gather crops where I did not scatter seed? Well, then you should have deposited my money in the bank, and I would have received it all back with interest when I returned. Now take the money away from him and give it to the one who has ten thousand coins. For to every person who has something, even more will be given, and he will have more than enough; but the person who has nothing, even the little that he has will be taken away from him. As for this useless servant — throw him outside in the darkness; there he will cry and gnash his teeth."

The Gospel of the Lord.

51 — PRAISE TO YOU, O CHRIST.

52 — There may be many ways to interpret this parable.

53 — But let's say the gold coins represent faith or discipline.

54 — Someone who has much faith and invests it wisely will gain more faith.

55 — And someone who exercises a little discipline will build more discipline.

56 — But someone who has faith but does not participate in a community of faith may lose what faith she or he has.

57 — And one who exercises no discipline will be left without any self-control at all.

58 — Perhaps this is a reason to practice a Lenten discipline.

59 — The season of Lent is nearly over.

60 — We challenge you tonight to pick up that Lenten discipline you may have dropped.

61 — Or start one if you had not previously chosen one.

62 — Then pray that we may be found faithful in small matters

63 — so that we may be given the chance to be faithful in larger matters.

64 — So that we may be able to keep the covenant spoken to Jeremiah.

65 — I WILL BE YOUR GOD AND YOU WILL BE MY PEOPLE.

66 — WATCH AND PRAY.

67 — We are at the foot of the cross.

Maundy Thursday
Courage

Readings
Exodus 12:1-14
Hebrews 10:32-39
Mark 14:12-26
Psalm 116:10-17

1 — WATCH AND PRAY.

2 — These are the words of our Savior to his disciples as he went to pray in the garden. It was the night he was betrayed to his enemies.

3 — WATCH AND PRAY.

4 — This has been our call to you this season of Lent as we have reflected once again upon that final week Christ walked the earth.

5 — WATCH AND PRAY.

6 — We have spoken of many things we need to follow Christ.

7 — We need self-knowledge, to identify ourselves as children of God who need not fear physical loss.

8 — We need daily repentance, to confess our own shortcomings lest we judge our neighbors.

9 — We need to grow in faith to become sturdy and strong so that at maturity our faith will bear good gifts to help others grow.

10 — We need patience, not to rush the will of God and to let his plan work in due season.

11 — And we need discipline to remain faithful and keep God's covenant.

12 — But now we are in the midst of Holy Week.

13 — It is the week we commemorate the darkest deeds in human history.

14 — This past Sunday, we celebrated Christ's triumphant entry into Jerusalem.

15 — Hosannas ring out.

16 — "Blessed is he who comes in the name of the Lord!" shouted the people.

17 — But Jesus quietly rode through the crowd, sitting on a young donkey.

18 — How many of these people would later call for Jesus' death?

19 — Their cries of "Hosanna!" turned to angry shouts of "Crucify him!"

20 — What would Jesus have been thinking that day?

21 — Did Jesus know he would die by the end of the week?

22 — How did the Son of God face that knowledge as people sang his praises?

23 — The only way any of us face unbearable circumstances: with courage.

24 — WATCH AND PRAY.

25 — On the way to Jerusalem, Jesus told his disciples no less than three times that he was going to die.

26 — But the disciples were not able to understand.

27 — As far as they were concerned, they were simply going to Jerusalem for the Passover festival.

28 — They were looking forward to eating the meal and hearing the story of the first Passover.

29 — A reading from the book of Exodus.

> *The Lord spoke to Moses and Aaron in Egypt: "This month is to be the first month of the year for you. Give these instructions to the whole community of Israel: On the tenth day of this month each man must choose either a lamb or a young goat for his household. If his family is too small to eat a whole animal, he and his next-door neighbor may share an animal, in proportion to the number of people and the amount that each person can eat. You may choose either a sheep or a goat, but it must be a one-year-old male without any defects. Then, on the evening of the fourteenth day of the month, the whole community of Israel will kill the animals. The people are to take some of the blood and put it on the doorposts and above*

the doors of the houses in which the animals are to be eaten. That night the meat is to be roasted, and eaten with bitter herbs and with bread made without yeast. Do not eat any of it raw or boiled, but eat it roasted whole including the head, the legs, and the internal organs. You must not leave any of it until morning; if any is left over, it must be burned. You are to eat it quickly, for you are to be dressed for travel, with your sandals on your feet and your walking stick in hand. It is the Passover festival to honor me, the Lord.

"On that night I will go through the land of Egypt, killing every firstborn male, both human and animal, and punishing all the gods of Egypt. I am the Lord. The blood on the doorposts will be a sign to mark the houses in which you live. When I see the blood, I will pass over you and will not harm you when I punish the Egyptians. You must celebrate this day as a religious festival to remind you of what I, the Lord, have done. Celebrate it for all time to come."

Here ends the reading.

30 — The Passover, then, is a festival of remembering.

31 — The Israelites were to remember their slavery in Egypt.

32 — More importantly, they were to remember the miraculous way in which God delivered them out of slavery.

33 — Passover was a time to look back at the courage of their ancestors.

34 — It was only the hope of a better life that gave the Israelites the courage to brave the wilderness.

35 — Perhaps this was the memory that made Jesus desire to celebrate the Passover one last time.

36 — Maybe even Christ needed this memory, this hope, to give him the courage he needed to face his coming suffering.

37 — WATCH AND PRAY.

38 — A reading from the letter to the Hebrews.

> *Remember how it was with you in the past. In those days, after God's light had shone on you, you suffered many things, yet were not defeated by the struggle. You were at times publicly insulted and mistreated and at other times you were ready to join those who were being treated in this way. You shared the sufferings of prisoners, and when all your belongings were seized, you endured your loss gladly, because you knew that you possessed something much better, which would last forever. Do not lose your courage, then, because it brings with it a great reward. You need to be patient, in order to do the will of God and receive what he promises. For, as the scripture says, "Just a little while longer, and he who is coming will come; he will not delay. My righteous people, however, will believe and live; but if any of them turns back, I will not be pleased with him."*
>
> *We are not people who turn back and are lost. Instead, we have faith and are saved.*

Here ends the reading.

39 — We are not people who turn back and are lost.

40 — There were any number of times for Jesus to turn back.

41 — From the tempting in the desert to his triumphant entry into Jerusalem, he had a choice to stop what he was doing.

42 — But he would not turn back.

43 — He did not lose his courage and he received a great reward.

44 — At first glance, it seems Jesus' reward was a cross.

45 — But Jesus also had patience to do God's will.

46 — And he endured the suffering to achieve the greatest reward:

47 — eternal life.

48 — Not only for himself,

49 — but for all people.

50 — WATCH AND PRAY.

51 — A reading from the Holy Gospel according to Saint Mark.

52 — GLORY TO YOU, O LORD.

53 — *On the first day of the Festival of Unleavened Bread, the day the lambs for the Passover meal were killed, Jesus' disciples asked him, "Where do you want us to go and get the Passover meal ready for you?"*

Then Jesus sent two of them with these instructions: "Go into the city, and a man carrying a jar of water will meet you. Follow him to the house he enters, and say to the owner of the house: 'The Teacher says, "Where is the room where my disciples and I will eat the Passover meal?" ' Then he will show you a large upstairs room, fixed up and furnished, where you will get everything ready for us."

The disciples left, went to the city, and found everything just as Jesus had told them; and they prepared the Passover meal.

When it was evening, Jesus came with the twelve disciples. While they were at the table eating, Jesus said, "I tell you that one of you will betray me — one who is eating with me."

The disciples were upset and began to ask him, one after the other, "Surely you don't mean me, do you?"

Jesus answered, "It will be one of you twelve, one who dips his bread in the dish with me. The Son of Man will die as the Scriptures say he will; but how terrible for that man who will betray the Son of Man! It would have been better for that man if he had never been born!"

While they were eating, Jesus took a piece of bread, gave a prayer of thanks, broke it, and gave it to his disciples. "Take it," he said, "this is my body."

Then he took a cup, gave thanks to God, and handed it to them; and they all drank from it. Jesus said, "This is my blood which is poured out for many, my blood which seals God's covenant. I tell you, I will never again drink this wine until the day I drink the new wine in the Kingdom of God."

Then they sang a hymn and went out to the Mount of Olives.

The Gospel of the Lord.

54 — PRAISE TO YOU, O CHRIST.

55 — This is the night we commemorate the betrayal of Christ.

56 — Jesus instituted a sacramental meal to remember this night.

57 — It is easy to forget the suffering this meal represents.

58 — But soon after the meal was eaten, Jesus was handed over to his enemies,

59 — betrayed in the garden by one of his closest friends.

60 — And Peter, the rock upon which Christ would build his church, vowed he would never deny Jesus.

61 — But within 24 hours, he was weeping bitterly over having done exactly that.

62 — The questioning, the beating, the humiliation,

63 — and finally, the cross.

64 — The body, broken on a cross, given for us.

65 — The blood flowing from undeserved wounds, shed for us.

66 — It is a courageous act to eat this bread and to drink from this cup.

67 — Let us claim this courage and join together for this holy meal.

68 — WATCH AND PRAY.

69 — As we touch the cross.